The Real China Beach

A Beach Surrounded by War

RJ Heurung

Library of Congress Control Number: 2024914373

ISBN
978-1-964982-01-4 (Paperback)
978-1-964982-02-1 (eBook)

We were the unwilling,
Led by the unqualified,
to do the unnecessary,
to the undeserving,
for the ungrateful.

I believe it was 2017 at our class of 1967 reunion you were kind enough to gift me a signed copy of your book "China Beach" and I thank you.

My husband is not a person who reads books often. Every winter since the fall of 2017 I have set your book on his table to peruse.

I have been dedicated to this task. Hubs was unable to serve due to a metal plate in his leg. So many of our friends served during the Viet Nam conflict/war.

This was the winter he finally picked your book to review/read!

He was so impressed. The book is now on its 3rd loan out. With strict instructions that is a signed copy and must be returned to Jo Ann(me).

Some things just simply take time and if it is important, you wait out the time it takes.

At one time I also had another book you compiled which I gave to classmate who served.

China Beach book has a few more friends of ours to reach.

I did not know you in high school but through reunions we became friends. I am so happy we finally met.

I thank for your service in Viet Nam, I thank you for ongoing service to all Viet Nam vets. Taking care of Military Cemetary's every summer for years, spreading the story of your service and continued support.

It pleases me. to follow you on Facebook through the adventures of gold mining, your new abode and Rocco.

You are a person that should be in the Tech Hall of Fame.

Blessings my friend and thank you!

Jo Ann Heuerman-Nystrom

Table of Contents

About the China Beach Cover Photo

I captured this photo in May 1968. I didn't realize until a few years ago that this was the month that US casualties peaked at 2,417. It's likely some of the men on this photo never came home alive. This is the real China Beach.

I remember standing on the shore of China Beach looking east towards America. Imagining if I could fly I knew I could navigate home, like a homing pigeon. Then I started thinking about how far over the horizon I would have to fly, I realized then that America was under my feet.

Now I felt even further from home.

My tour in Vietnam changed my life forever. I have dedicated my life helping veterans in any way I can. I documented my tour of Vietnam through photos, as my dad did in World War II. Sharing my photos and experiences with veterans and the public is an honor. "I am forever honored, for I have marched with heroes!"

Graduates Construction Electrician Class "A" School,
February 1968, Port Hueneme California

Orders to Vietnam after completing Electrician school, weapons training, and SERE (survival, resistance, evasion, escape).

Q: What Are US Navy Seabees? A Naval Infantry
Naval Infantry Flag

NOT SEALS...NOT MARINES...FILLING THE GAP BETWEEN

THE USE OF THE BATTALION INFANTRY FLAG IS MOSTLY LIMITED TO BATTALIONS OF SHIPS LANDING PARTIES AND ORINIZATIONS OF NAVAL SHORE ACTIVITIES

PARTICULARILY CONSTRUCTION BATTALIONS OF THE LEGENDARY NAVY SEABEES.

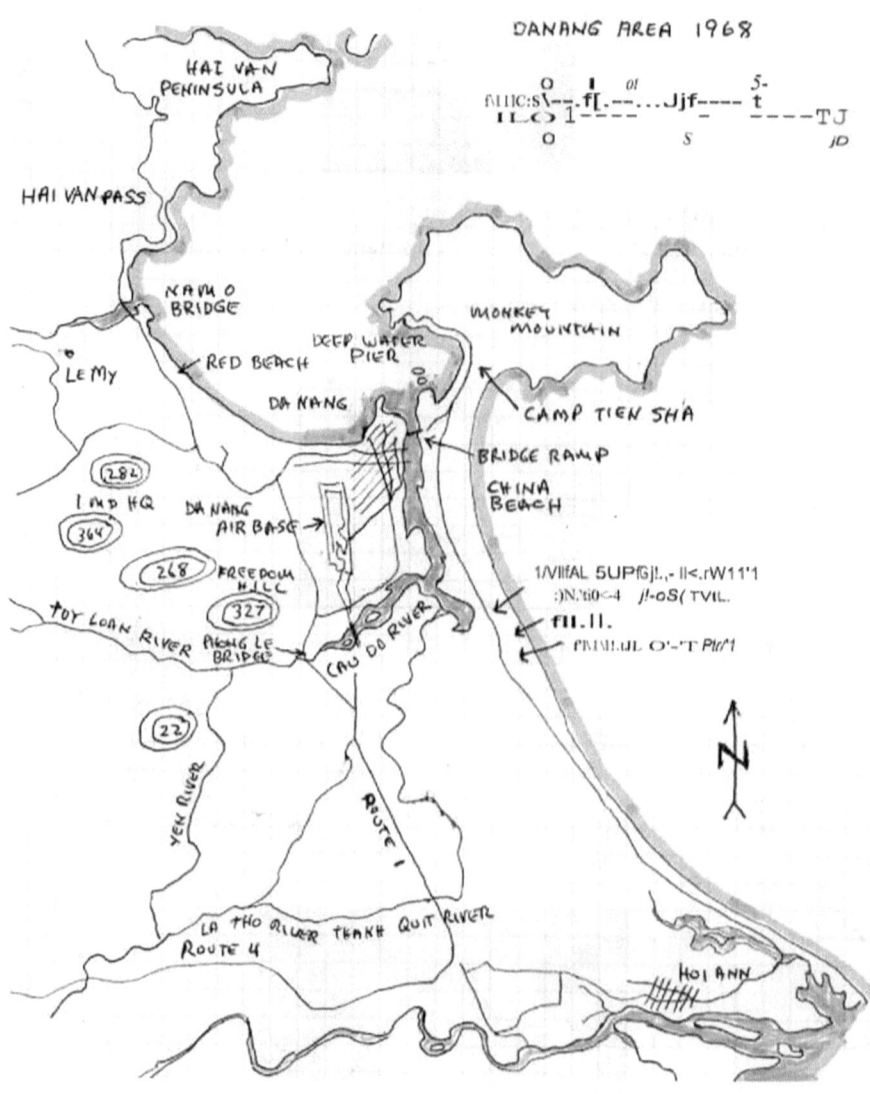

My childhood.

I grew up in a small town in the midwest. I attending a catholic grade school for 9 years. For fun we would play games like cowboys and Indians, stalking each other. I hated having to be the one to have to play dead. We we're kind of serious about this game and sometimes used bee bee guns.

We would hunt and fish. We had a family of 9 and hunting and fishing was fun but serious. We had a lot of meals of fish, squirrel, rabbit, pheasant, grouse, waterfowl and venison. We had to conserve ammo by being a good shot. I had paper routes, shoveled snow, mowed lawns, worked on farms, and found lots of ways to make money. I was a cub scout and aged my way into boy scouts. I loved scouting and had numerous merit badges. I was on a civil defense team and helped clean up after storms.

My Grandfather was in WW 1 and my father was in the infantry in WW2.

I always had nothing but respect for Veterans and the Military. I was due to graduate from high school in June of 1967. There was a draft at this time with high school seniors required to register. If your parents had enough money you could get a collage deferment by getting you into college. Some talked about fleeing to Canada or Mexico. I wanted to go into the Military, and wanted to go to Vietnam. I wanted a piece of the action. I thought serving my country was the right thing to do. There wasn't much opposition to the war at this time.I was 17 at this time and my Dad wouldn't let me enlist in the Army or Marines. Dad didn't want me in combat. Someone told me about the Seabees. The Seabees comes from the term Construction Battalion's. The Navy had an early entry program, where I could sign up for before graduating. This would take me off the draft list and give me some choice of the trade I wanted to learn. This would also give me a high chance of ending up in a combat zone. I enlisted in the Navy as a Construction recruit instead of a Seaman recruit. My Dad didn't realize I chose combat construction duty. I graduated from high school on a Friday and was on a train heading for Great lakes Illinois Saturday Morning.

I didn't like high school and barely graduated. However, when I took aptitude test for the Military I scored high, especially in math. I wanted to be heavy equipment operator in the Seabees but the Navy decided I had two much of a brain so I was trained as a Construction Electrician.

Navy recruit training is the same for Seaman and Construction recruits. Getting your hair buzzed off, new stiff moth ball smelling uniforms, learning how to shave, getting humiliated in inspections, dumpster watches, standing in formation in the hot sun for hours, marching, and endless Naval classes. The only thing I liked about boot camp was the good food.

From boot camp I headed to Port Hueneme California for Construction Electrician "A" school. Half of our day was spent in the class room. The rest of the day we we're learning power line construction. We we're issued climbing boots and gaffs. We were issued files and taught how to sharped gaffs. Climbing 45 foot poles was scary at first but you had to learn. Some hurt themselves by sliding down a pole, scraping the insides of their arms and legs. Some scraped the side of their faces and some would jab a gaff into their foot. A couple refused to try and we're transferred to the regular navy. I could see that this work was dangerous and demanding. It was the challenge I was looking for and I got to like it. Climbing got to actually be fun. We also learned how to rewind motors and splice lead shielded phone cables. We learned how to wire and operate telephone switch boards. We learned electrical theory. We we're tried and tested. A few failed and we're transferred to the regular Navy.

Next it was off to Camp Pendleton for weapons and sere training (survival, evasion, resistance, escape). I recall the steep hills scaled getting to and from the firing rang. We were pushed hard and some collapsed. A chopper flew them out and you never seen them again. I hated firing 5 round busts from an m-14. My shoulder was black and blue for a while.

My departure:

I sat peering out my 5th floor hotel room overlooking a busy street in San Diego. What a strange place this was. I was never in hotel in such a large city. The street below was bustling with activity.

I pulled the window up to let in a blast of city life. Hello to the hot morning sun, the big city odors, the honking horns and sirens.

Hunger and confusion started my day.

I could have stayed at Coronado. I would at least get fed. The little money I had went to a bible salesman. It's a beautiful bible, and it probably was a good deal. I must have thought it was fate that the last thing I give my parents is a bible.

My flight to Vietnam didn't leave for another 30 hours. I rewired the TV so I wouldn't have to put quarters in it. The room was paid for and I had my bus ticket, but I'm flat broke. I couldn't go back to Coronado Island because I don't have money for the ferry boat.

By mid afternoon I had to try something for food. I started walking these strange city streets. What do homeless do? Do they eat out of dumpsters? I could never beg.

I came across a free lunch sign on a small chapel. We had to sing and pray a couple hours before we we're fed. Most of the guys seemed to be homeless. I was wearing nice clothes and was clean, and was getting weird stares from these guys. By the time I got out of their it was almost dark. I was glad to get back to my room. What an ordeal to go through for a meal. I was thinking this was my last meal in the US.

The next morning I woke up hungry again, but knew I would get fed on the plane. I had to get to Norton Air Force base.

By evening I was in the 727. They added an extra row of seats and the isles were narrow. This jet was already hot, smoky, and crowded. We had a 30 hour flight ahead of us. We finally took off and I finally got something to eat that night.

It seemed like the flight took 3 days. No one was talking, we we're all occupied with what might be coming. Once we boarded the jet, there was no turning back. We passed through numerous sunrise and sunsets. I was sick from cigarette smoke, but knew I couldn't show it. I had to stay focused. I knew I didn't have a chance of making it back unless I used my training and wits. I kept thinking of what kind of weapon I would carry. I was hoping for an M-14.

No one wanted the M16, we knew it was junk because they jammed on the practice range. I was also hoping for a M- 60 machine gun or M-79 grenade launcher. I was wondering about where I'd be sleeping that night.

I had pain in my mid section from hunger and fear. Fear really set in when it was announced on the PA "we will be landing at Danang Air Base in an hour. We are entering hostile air space and may be fired upon. We will have escorts soon. May god be with us".

We landed hard at Danang Air Base. When we got to the end of the runway the jet made a left too fast. The right wing hit the ground. The pilot then put the power on and taxied fast. We pulled up to the loading area with brakes and reverse thrusters. Doors flew open before we even stopped. We departed the plane fast and orderly. As I stepped out of door smells of another world hit me. It was a hot, humid, cloudy day. The familiar airport smells were mixed with the hot wind off the China Sea. As I rushed off the jet the 1st thing we seen was a few hundred weary looking troops ready to board, looking at us as if they felt sorry for us. Most of them had their field greens on.

We were massed to a loading area where gray school busses we're waiting. It didn't take long to get from the jet to Busses. We could here small arms fire and out-going artillery around the airbase. The driver took off like we were late. He shouted to everyone to keep their heads down.

The bus headed us for Camp Tien Sha. We made petty good time until we got to the Danang Bridges. The bus was in stop & go traffic with Vietnamese all around us. We had no weapons and our dress whites on. We limped along towards the bridges thru heat and fear. We felt like sitting ducks. The driver kept saying "I hate this job".

We could sense from the stares of the locals that we were not welcome. Some of them looked like the wanted to kill us, even the old Mama Sons and kids. We finally got over the bridge and headed on to Tien Sha Peninsula. The driver announced we were almost there.

The sound of shattering glass announced us to the war. A burst of small arms fire hit the back of the bus. Screams of pain, anger, and fear became familiar to me as of that day. Bright dress white uniforms covered with bright red blood is one of the scenes I will never forget.

Red Beach, my first day in Vietnam.

Four US ships of Amphibious Task Force 76 appeared off Danang, Vietnam, on March 8, 1965. Intermittent rain and up to 4-foot waves delayed the landing at Red Beach 2 for about an hour. With the arrival of the Marines and the escalation of the air campaign, America's military role in Vietnam crossed the line from advise and assist to offensive warfare. Called Red Beach because of the colors reflected over the water at dawn and sunset, it is now considered a clean, peaceful tourist attraction about 9 miles from Da Nang's city center.

Throughout this book I'll be inserting guestbook entries from the "Military Memories Guest Book".

10/22/2009
Name: Jerry Weitzmane
Location: Red Beach

Comments: As an MCB 58er I was at Red Beach in 1966–67 and 1967–68 I remember like yesterday when our base was attacked. It was on a Sunday about 9:45 p.m. It was one of the three times I was drunk. Boy, did I sober up fast… and no hangover! However, that incident wasn't as scary as almost drowning in the South China Sea trying to ride a surfboard in Hoi An. The water was like glass, but there was an undertow or a riptide. I was told a Korean Marine saved my life.

Red Beach perimeter bunker facing Hai Van Pass.
This area was lit up with flares every night, to

Philco-Ford plant at the base of Hai Van Pass, invaders every night.

Freedom Hill, Danang Vietnam.
Bob Hope traveled to Vietnam annually from 1964 to 1972, bringing
dozens of stars with him over the years

The Rock Pit, where there was frequent electrical work.

1968 Dodge Power Wagon, my favorite truck.
As an electrician in the Seabees I had to be ready to get anywhere.

A valley of big guns.

Behind mines and wire, The M107 175 mm self-propelled gun

1st Marine Division HQ

1st Marine Division Headquarters Company I Corps
near Danang Vietnam 1968

8/25/1998 Name: Tran Huong Que From Vietnam Comments: I was crying looking at your photos. I would like to say thank you to all the American soldiers, the Australian, and others who had helped the South Vietnamese army fighting against the invasion and expansion of the Communists from the north. I don't know what else to say but pray to God. I am now living in Australia. I miss and love Vietnam so much. I hope Vietnam soon will have freedom.

Monday, 11/27/2000 Name: Phung Location: California Comments: Dear Vietnam Vets, I grew up in Da Nang. For as long as I could remember, at night the VC would disrupt our lives with artillery shells and other scare tactics. It was your presence that kept them in check. Because of you, I was able to enjoy a safer, happier childhood. For that, I am extremely grateful to you! Please always remember that what you fought for, freedom and democracy, were worthy and noble causes in my eyes. Because of your work, the seeds of freedom were passed on to me, and I am today able to embrace this freedom and grow to my fullest. What a tremendous gift you have given me

1998-09-22 Name: Dinh Vo The Real China Beach 67 Originally from Vietnam, moved to US in 1982 Comments: Oh God, It reminded me right away once I looked at the pictures, especially the China Beach. I was about 10 or 11 years old in 1968 and went to My Khe Beach almost every weekend. In the picture Da Nang, that Jeep belonged to my brother, was parked in front of his house at 53 Phan Dinh Phung, District I. My brother was a MP officer (Military Police) for South Vietnam and worked for District I MP Station

10/09/2001 Name: Andrew Balus Location: Newport RI
Comments: I found this site while looking for info on the TV show 'China Beach', which much to my dismay. Is no longer on The History Channel every night. I would just like to thank you so much for the photos. I've never seen images that seemed so "real" before. Sure I've seen even graphic TV news reels, but not actual Veterans photos. As I get older (I'm 29) I'm slowly realizing how tragic war really is, and sincerely hope you somehow got through it all the best you could. I have nothing but the utmost respect for all US service men/women, and would just like to give a big "thank you" from the bottom of my heart. I do realize that freedom has a price, and do appreciate all you've done for our wonderful country. Godspeed, and god bless

Sat, Apr 14 2012, 18:25, CDT | L Graves | Location: United States | U.S. Navy Combat Photographer (NAV-4V; Det. Charlie).
Thanks for this web site and the postings. It brings back memories [Many are sad, as reflected in the ones here].
Rather we like those memories or not; they are the facts, the history. I would be interested in hearing from other
U.S. Navy and U.S. Marine photographers of that era. Good Luck To ALL. Thanks for your Military service

1/31/2013 Name: Paul Mears **Comments**: I was at Camp Tien Sha 1968-1969 with Tien Sha Security (TSP) charged with perimeter security. We experienced rocket attacks and long tedious watches. The ammo dump got hit and went off for days, 500lb bombs make quite a racket. In-country R&R at China Beach surfing the waves and watching the big red Asian sun come up out of the China sea. Ron Washington was a pal who worked hard for his race. Fellow security pals were big Jim Kelly from NY, Paul Sustin from El Lay and many others. I would love to hear from anyone at that time. We guarded the Deep Water Piers and many towers to safeguard our fellow servicemen. I'm proud to have served and grateful to all the vets who answered their coun

10/24/2000 Name: Michael Leap Location: Blue Springs MO Comments: Thanks for posting your work. It's good for me to see your pictures of you today but I've learned over the years 'since' I can identify best when I can visualize how 'we' looked then. So thanks also for posting the picture of the good lookin' kid. I'm pretty sure you and I are very close in age. I became 22 aboard ship in 8/65 enroute to the Danang area. Good old improvising Marines sure policed up the area after I left.

China Beach, Monkey Mtn (the road!). Your pictures are a real treasure; thanks for sharing them.

02//3/1998 Name: Joseph Nguyen From: Stockton, California Comments: I was born in Hue and grew up in Danang by China Beach, Monkey Mountain, Tien Sa, An Hai, Son Cha… area (just one of those war children). You have great pictures, those are very familiar to me, I went back there July 1997 to see my family, I hiked Monkey Mountain, Marble Mountain, China Beach… Things changed, the country is still beautiful and poor. I respect and thank all of you who serviced in Nam, it meant a lot to some people… God bless you.

View of Monkey Mountain
from 1ˢᵗ Marine HQ,
where our journey will end

Name: Michael I. Phelps, US Marines
Location: McAllen Texas

Comments: Long story made short, I got to the 'Nam in early August 1969. On or about August 12, 1969, while still at First Marine Division HQ, I was in my first combat when the HQ was attacked by NVA/VC ground troops, rockets, etc. The last rocket fired by the enemy hit within a few yards of my fighting position. We later collected the enemy dead and transported them to a location near the front gate. The dead enemies were thrown off the trucks where me and some other FNGs lined them up in rows where we searched them for intel. A few days later after I went to NAC after which I went out to An Hoa Combat Base. Later to Hill 65, then Hill 52, then later to Hill 65 again until I left the 'Nam.

Hoi Ann ROK Marine Base, South Vietnam, 1968

Deadly nights for those trying to over run the perimitor.
Hội An Base Camp, Republic of Korea Marine Corps (ROKMC)
land Army of the Republic of Vietnam (ARVN)

1999-11-05
Name: Alan Case

From Milliken, Colorado, now Wellford, South Carolina

Comments: Those who don't understand say we are to "Put it behind us" or "Forget about it. It's over. It's been 30 years." BS! What they don't understand is that no matter where we came from, what our background was, what color our skin is, the experiences from that year or those years in that country have changed us forever, have made us what we are today—for the better or the worse! For myself, I never want to forget. I want always to remember the names and faces of those that I lay face down with during a mortar attack, hoping it would quit soon. Those that I shared a poncho liner with during the monsoons to keep from freezing our asses off. Those that I got so fu——— drunk with that we couldn't walk or crawl back to the hooch. Those that shared stories of family, hometown, girlfriends, and wives. I never want to forget. Those of you who know, know exactly what I mean. Those men—although most of us were no more than boys—were closer than any brother could ever be (my opinion). I will always remember those who came home and those who were brought home. SSG 11/B; B 1/11; 1/5 Inf Div (Mech) Quang Tri 68–69; 70–71

01/21/2012
Name: Rick Hoover, US Army
Location: Pasadena, Texas

Comments: 282nd Assault Helicopter Company, "the Black Cats,"
January '69–January'70. Two jobs: crew chief on a fire truck with the
MAG-16, door gunner / Hueys (mostly medevacs and mail runs). The
Alley Cats were the real combat vets. My idea of paradise: the extinct
volcano—a naval radar base—Cu Lao Re Island (now Ly Son, I think)
a few miles off shore. Flying in beside the cliffs and waterfalls, plunging
to the clear blue sea will ease your mind. Hello to any of my MAG-16
buddies. You guys couldn't buy hard liquor! So I shared my rations
-)! And to you Army buds, I'm too far gone to remember names, but
I think of you all and can see your faces still. I hope you have had a
good life. I certainly have. And those who gave all, see you again on
the other side.

We're south of Marble Mountain and drew fire often in this area. It was part of our job. Good thing there was always air cover like the F4 on the top of the photo.

China Beach is just to the north of Marble Mountain.

The road from Hoi An to the China Beach compound greeted us with snipers and ambushes, but we we're always covered by aircraft like the F4 Phantom flying overhead.

China Beach generating plant near the entrance.

Sky Crane over China Beach, Vietnam 1968

China Beach USO Rest and Relaxaton Center
Republic of South Vietnam 1968

"To Millions of American viewers, China Beach was merely the backdrop for a hit TV show. But it was dead real to thousands of GIs, offering them a rare respite from battle. The Vietcong used the place as a terrorist base. Later, it launched the boat people. Today, China Beach, Vietnam, is one of the most luxurious beaches on this earth."

—Ron Gluckman

I captured this photo in May 1968. I didn't realize until a few years ago that this was the month that US casualties peaked at 2,417. It's likely some of the men on this photo never came home alive. This is the Real China Beach.

Beer and BBQ in the cool shade of the trees, but the hot sand and scorching sun could burn you. It was Dangerous life guard duty with sharks, jelly fish and rip tides.

Comments: USAF at TACC-NS on Monkey '68–'69. Thought it might be some of my crew in China Beach pics. I would take whole crew down after getting off night shift, and we played jungle ball and touch football (feet wet, tackle was OK) and we ate dogs-burgers and drank beer until we went back for night shift. Also ran into sea snakes in the water, and once, some nurses came out from a hospital ship wearing bikinis, instantly there was a 50-foot clear circle of several hundred guys just staring at them while they got settled in the center. Then a low-flying helo came by and circled around them several times but finally left. After lots of guys attempted to hit on them, the girls finally had enough and left.

Consoling each other before returning to the bush.

01/13/2010
Name: Rich Doc Raitano, Army Medic
Comments: In-country December 1967–September 1968 Fourth
Battalion, Third Infantry Regiment (Old Guard) Eleventh LIB,
Americal Division. I spent my first three months rotating between
Bravo and Delta off of LZ Sue. Aid station on Hill 54 and LZ Bronco.
In March, was sent to Chu Lai as a casualty reporter for the battalion
and TF Barker. I evaluated, assessed, and interviewed the wounded,
then headed to GR to assess and evaluate the KIAs, phone in a report
to S-2, and send a hard copy to the battalion and brigade by mail. I
spent 3 weeks in Da Nang at the NSA Hospital, and it has just occurred
to me that I may have been sent to do a little R&R as there were only
1 or 2 of our grunts in the hospital. I spent much time on the beach. I
have a photo of myself surrounded by kids with Monkey Mountain in
the background.

4th of July 1968, party at China Beach, one of the three times I could actually enjoy the beach. I could smile and relax here.

What were we thinking ?

I remember standing on the shore of China Beach looking east towards America. Imagining if I could fly I knew I could navigate home, like a homing pigeon. Then I started thinking about how far over the horizon I would have to fly, I realized then that America was under my feet. Now I felt even further from home.

A time to reflect.

Breif enjoyment at beautiful China Beach.

Monkey Mountain in the background.

4th of July party China Beach 1968

After 48 years I can't remember these men's
names. I'm sure they won't be offended.

There were sail boats we could use at the China Beach R&R Center. We had to beware of sharks and jellyfish.

The USO had a couple of sail boats we could use. I went out on one and we we're escorted back to shore by about a dozen ten foot sharks. They didn't leave until we we're in like 2 feet of water.

A couple of officers attending our China Beach
party and entertained a couple of the locals

These officers flew in and partied with us. They
wouldn't let anyone get near these women.

I really wanted to fly this thing. It was the booze talking.

I don't think it was this chopper everyone was interested in.

A breif stop behind the China Beach PX.

Choppers land frequently behind the China Beach Exchange.

China Beach Compound, behind the PX

China Beach Exchange

10/09/2001
Name: Andrew Balus

Location: Newport, Rhode Island

Comments: I found this site while looking for info on the TV show *China Beach*, which much to my dismay is no longer on the History Channel every night. I would just like to thank you so much for the photos. I've never seen images that seemed so "real" before. Sure, I've seen even graphic TV news reels, but not actual veterans' photos. As I get older (I'm 29), I'm slowly realizing how tragic war really is, and sincerely hope you somehow got through it all the best you could. I have nothing but the utmost respect for all US service men/women and would just like to give a big thank-you from the bottom of my heart. I do realize that freedom has a price, and do appreciate all you've done for our wonderful country. Godspeed and God bless.

Heavy rain on China Beach from the building I worked in.

The China Beach Barber Shop. Vietnamese barbers gave a shoulder message and shave with a straight razor as part of the haircut. I would have rather skipped the shave, but wouldn't want to get them upset.

If you explore current maps you can see the fuel tanks on China Beach.

Looking east, just over ridge is China Beach.
The building on the left had pool tables.

We tried to grow tomatoes but only got big plants.

Korean engineers I had the privilege of serving
with. They were kind intelligent people.

Office duty was good
after we had air conditioning.

I wanted to be a heavy-equipment operator in the Seabees, but had too much of a brain, so they made me an electrician. I was doing a lot of drafting and estimating, so when we went out into the bush, we could get in and out as fast as possible.

Hard at work, no AC until a month before I left.

My desk when I first got to Vietnam.

My desk after almost a year.

We had to be ready for invaders, even during the day.

I left Vietnam in April of 1969 before his addition to our office building was done.

Buildings on China Beach not completed before I left in April 1969.

Treats from home.

A Vietnamese woman who worked in our office was very kind and respectfull.

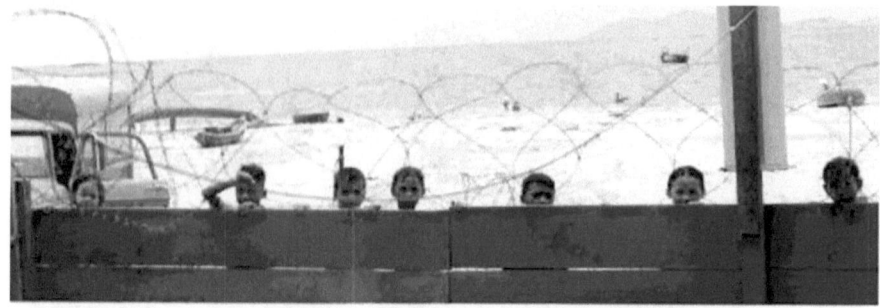

As part of a volunteer civic action program, this small compound was where we would treat children's minor injuries. Infected wounds were lanced, squeezed out, and stitched up without anything to ease the pain. The tears would flow, but these kids would never cry. They always thanked us through the pain and tears.

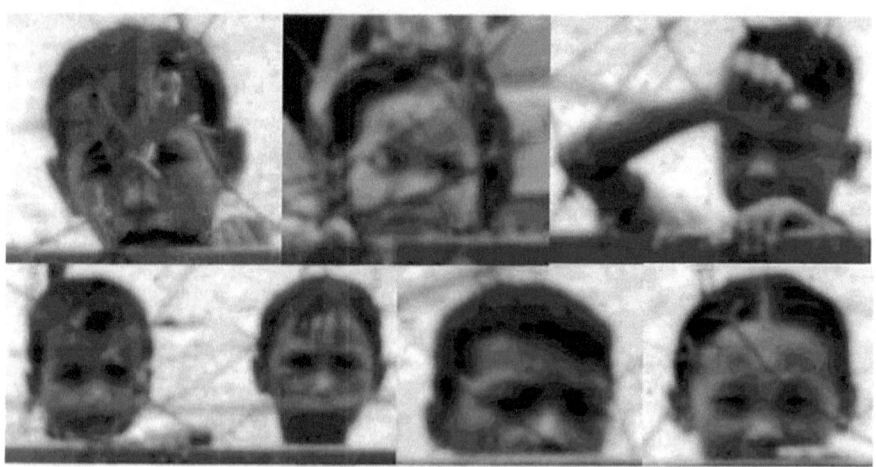

1998-02-23
Name: Joseph Nguyen

From Stockton, California

Comments: I was born in Hue and grew up in Da Nang by China Beach, Monkey Mountain, Tien Sa, An Hai, Son Cha area (just one of those war children). You have great pictures; those are very familiar to me. I went back there July 1997 to see my family. I hiked Monkey Mountain, Marble Mountain, China Beach. Things changed; the country is still beautiful and poor. I respect and thank all of you who serviced in'Nam; it meant a lot to some people. God bless you.

A Vietnamese school north of China Beach.

No clue who had these kids' attention or how the '56 Chevy got there.

The busy Danang riverfront.

8/25/1998
Name: Tran Huong Que
From Vietnam

Comments: I was crying looking at your photos. I would like to say thank you to all the American soldiers, the Australian, and others who had helped the South Vietnamese army fighting against the invasion and expansion of the Communists from the north. I don't know what else to say but pray to God. I am now living in Australia. I miss and love Vietnam so much. I hope Vietnam soon will have freedom.

It was much too dangerous for this hospital
ship to stay here overnight.

Let's cross the bridge to the Da Nang side.

Lets head over to the Danang side.

Bland new tanks ready for action.

08/24/2009

Name: Mike Walsh, BM-3, USN; CHB-2E
Location: Haworth, New Jersey

Comments: Navy: Thank you for this wonderful depository of memories of a period long ago. Although most of the photos are of a time after my tour, things did not change all that much. Cargo Handling Battalion Two (CHB-2) arrived in Da Nang in April '65 with the Third Marines from Subic Bay and lived with them in tent city on the Da Nang AFB initially. We supervised the civilian stevedores on the inland piers and MSTS ships in the harbor. In 1965 we were still using greenbacks before the switch to MPC script (funny money). For the first 3–4 months we lived in local hotels, APLs, APAs, eventually at Camp Tien Sha. We had no idea that in another 4 months we'd be part of a force of several thousand to be known as NSA Da Nang. I served in Da Nang from April '65–July '66 on the piers (T-Pier and Deepwater), Tien Sha Ramp, and the Riggers Loft. We arrived about 85 strong BMs, EOs, and SKs from Subic Bay, but most of the guys left before my extension kicked in. I've been searching the Internet many years but have not come across any of the ol' crew. So, "Mother" Tucker, Tuttle, "Stretch" Buchanan, Moncrief, Sims, King, and any of the other glorified "deck apes" out there, give me a shout! Thank you for your service, my brothers and sisters, and *welcome home.*

used with permission of Stanley Houlberg Jr

used with permission of Stanley Houlberg Jr.

used with permission of Stanley Houlberg Jr

The afternoon of February 27, 1969, Milton Shiparo offered to take the load of ammo we were scheduled to pick up at Bridge Ramp. Our enginemen were just finishing up repairs on a steering motor on board our boat that prevented us from sailing over to the bridge ramp to have the ammo loaded so we could set sail later that evening. Because of Milton's volunteering for that load, I am still here. I would have been in the pilot house at the time of the attack, preparing for my midwatch and leaving port.

The attack happened just after 2300, and the fire and explosions lasted close to midnight. I watched it from the lighterage dock, where all the LCUs and YFUs are tied up between trips. I believe only three men on the 78 survived. They had just returned from the EM club at Camp Tien Sha and were in the boat's galley when the attack happened. As I was told, there were three rockets fired at the boats. The first landed alongside the warehouses along the north side of the ramp; the second landed just behind both the 1500 and 78.

A crew member on my boat, the 74, told us he heard the man on watch in the pilot house of the 78 asking the HQ at the lighterage for permission to leave the loading area. That must have been just before the third rocket hit the 1500 and both boats went up. Black powder and projectiles were our usual load whenever we loaded up at the bridge ramp, and the 78 probably had over 300 tons on board. The 1500 probably had over 200 tons.

I didn't see the initial explosion, but I felt it from at least two miles away. By the time I made it up into our pilot house, the bridge ramp area was still exploding.

My middle daughter, Katie, went to Washington, DC, in 1998 for a high school outreach trip. She went to the Wall for me to look up Milton Shapiro's name. She took a shading, and when she brought it home to me and placed it in my hand, I had a strange feeling and chills. Later that evening I looked up Milton's name on the Vietnam Veterans Causality List web site and discovered that Katie had taken Milton's shading exactly 29 years to the day of the attack.

In my prayers I often remember Milton and the others who took my place that night. Thanks to their unselfish heroism I have enjoyed a wonderful life and have a wonderful family.

Thank you for this memorial to the YFU 78 and the LCU 1500. They were all good sailors and fine men. God bless our Vietnam veteran heroes!

Sincerely,
Stanley Houlberg Jr., QM3

used with permission of Stanley Houlberg Jr.

Name: Bob
Heurung
Location:
Arizona/Minnesota

Comments: The morning of this rocket attack I was one of the first] to get there after the explosion. It was right at the break of day. Two jets were slamming rockets into the rice paddies north of the bridges. More rockets could be coming. I was sent to survey the damage to the ship. As I got near the ship, I noticed a lot of pieces of flesh. Someone was gathering the pieces.

I climbed up the steep, flimsy gangway and was shocked as I reached the deck. I was hoping there might be survivors, but the only thing left was a thick layer of bloody mush covering everything. It was so red it hurt my eyes. I made a quick sketch of a square hole about eight feet wide in the center of the deck. Then I saw a puff of smoke coming from the gaping hole.

As I turned to retreat, I noticed about a dozen Marines in the hold staring up at me. I yelled smoke and everyone scattered. I came down off the gangway and ran for my pickup. Everyone was running away from the smoking vessel. I got in my truck and just cleared the end of the bridge when the second explosion blew.

I had to get back to China Beach and turn in my report. My commander told me everyone thought I was a goner when the second explosion went off. Everyone was glad to see I made it back. We got a report that 24 men were sleeping on the bow deck when the rocket hit. They were all turned into mush. No one ever mentions the second explosion when the explosives in the ship blew up. The rocket blew a hole in the deck, but the ship was still intact. Maybe this was a different rocket attack? There were many.

10/14/2010

Name: Bruce G Hoffman,
US Location: Maryville,
Missouri

Comments: I was one of 5 survivors on the YFU 78 the night of February 27, 1969. Four of us were playing cards in the mess decks, with one man watching. He and I had the midnight watch, and we were expecting to leave any minute. Charlie, our cook, was sitting beside me next to the starboard hatch when we were hit. He didn't make it, and the other four of us swam out the port hatch.

The boat sank in seconds, and the last to come out was the gunner's mate. He was in the PO3 compartment beside the port hatch. The 4 of us from the mess decks got to shore by the pilings near the ramps just before the gunner made it to shore.

My leg had a sizable chunk out of my thigh, and we were talking about what to do about it when our backload began to erupt. By then my leg was numb, and the gunner put me over his shoulder, and he and the 3 other ran.

I watched as our boat was blowing up. I remember a lot more, but there was a second or two between seeing my great hand of spades and all went black. I had been sitting in the bench by the starboard bulkhead at the mess deck table. I next was sitting in my partner's swivel chair, looking back at the torn starboard hatch and bulkhead, flames, smoke, and disappearing emergency lights.

Water was already up to my ankles before I stood up to see if my leg would work. During a brief yelling back and forth as to what to do, I had yelled to go out the port hatch and yelled for others to follow until I was underwater. I had yelled when I went under and was out of breath. Boot camp training kicked in, and I went up to the overhead between beams for air. When I pushed down and toward the hatch, my left foot stepped on the lip of the hatch. The hatch must have been blown open, and as I came out, I looked up and could see the surface.

I have always wondered about how that night went down. I have read several accounts of what some think happened. I can only account for the fact we didn't know anything was amiss and suddenly we were sinking and trying to survive.

Busy rice paddies on the outskirts of Danang

Busy rice paddies near the Danang bridges, also harbored the enemy
sneaking in rockets and mortars.

Monday, 11/27/2000
Name: Phung
Location: California

Comments: Dear Vietnam Vets, I grew up in Da Nang. For as long as I could remember, at night the VC would disrupt our lives with artillery shells and other scare tactics. It was your presence that kept them in check. Because of you, I was able to enjoy a safer, happier childhood. For that, I am extremely grateful to you!

Please always remember that what you fought for, freedom and democracy, were worthy and noble causes in my eyes. Because of your work, the seeds of freedom were passed on to me, and I am today able to embrace this freedom and grow to my fullest. What a tremendous gift you have given me!

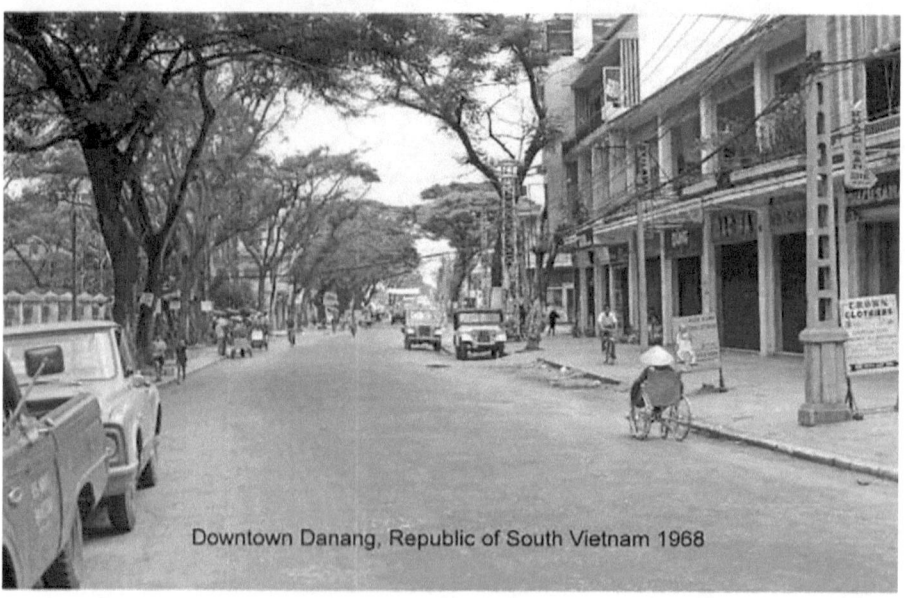

Downtown Danang, Republic of South Vietnam 1968

1998-09-22
Name: Dinh Vo

Originally from Vietnam, moved to US in 1982

Comments: Oh God, It reminded me right away once I looked at the pictures, especially the *China Beach*. I was about 10 or 11 years old in 1968 and went to My Khe Beach almost every weekend. In the picture *Da Nang*, that Jeep belonged to my brother, was parked in front of his house at 53 Phan Dinh Phung, District I. My brother was a MP officer (Military Police) for South Vietnam and worked for District I MP Station.

French architecture, upper-class home.

This must have been my rooky days. This was a dangerous place to turn my back to

One of the very few photos with me holding a weapon. My parents saw these photos before I did, and I wanted to make it look like I was in no danger. It looked that way, but I'm lucky to be alive.

We all had time guarding vehicles. The preceding day a GI was killed by a sniper at this very spot. There was still a lot of dried blood on the ground. Under the watchful eyes of a marine bunker and SEAL snipers I was hoping to draw fire.

The slums of Danang
using every bit of dry land.

The Danang outskirts were highly populated.
All dry ground was used.

Lowland dwelling in Danang, 1968.

The Danang Hotel.

Busy downtown Danang, all eyes on me.

A busy market.

Here we are on the outskirts of the Da Nang Air Base.

Duty at the Danang Mortuary at the Danang Air Base.

The steel grey warehouse baked in the Asian sun. The odor of jet fuel and death filled the 100 plus degree air. The sound of jets and helicopters shadowed the distant artillery and machine gun fire. As I enter the building I was shocked by the number of dead. A couple hundred body bags and sheet covered stretchers laid out in rows inside the door leading to the hello pad. It was hot, crowded and silent in this place. The hallway was lined by gurneys. White tag tied toes stuck out from under the sheets.

I entered the operating area occupied by about 20 morticians working in silence. Steel racks of black and clear body bags lined one side of the room. An assortment of naked mutilated soldiers lay still in a single row of about 20 tables. I broke the attention of a mortician. He took off his mucky rubber gloves and walked towards me, looking straight into eyes as if imagining me dead.

I told my business, to rearrange and add more over head lights and tables. He showed me around the maze of death. I took measurements and made sketches. He made it clear that his work or no ones could be interrupted.

"Stay out of our way and get this done fast."

A generator had to be repaired. We walked outside blasted by the heat and stench.

A row of walk in coolers had signs. TO BE EMBALMED, TO GO HOME. A huge stack of hundreds of aluminum coffins baked in the sun.

Images of this place will never leave my mind.

Da Nang Air Base.

A-6 Intruder takes off from
Danang Airport, Vietnam 1968

Marine F-4 Phantom
Danang Vietnam Airbase 1968

The ground shook as you could feel the roar
of these F-4 Phantoms taking off together.

F-4 Phantoms took off in pair

F4 Phantoms refuel and re-arm
Danang Airbase 1968

Danang Air Base under watch by 1st LAAM (1st Light Antiaircraft Missile Battalion)
deployed to Vietnam in 1965 providing air defense for the Marine Corps in the I Corps sector.

Marine HAWK missile position overlooking Danang Air Base, 1968

Department of Defense (USMC) photo A422857 [Public domain]

Name: Frederick L Marotta, USMC
From: Winchester, BOSTON, Massachusetts

Comments: Yes, many of us have put the slides and photos away. I enjoyed viewing your pics. You've got two that are close to my heart. The photos of the RF-4B, the Phantom with the RM on the tail and the number 21 on the nose. The other is the EA-6B, the plane with the hook (refuel probe) on the nose and the RM on the tail. These aircraft were from my squadron, VMCJ-1. J-1 was part of the MAG-11 First Marine Aircraft Wing. We were at the Da Nang Air Base. I served from November '68 to December '69. Semper fi. First LA AM "Hawk" Battalion (Marine Anti-Aircraft Missile Battalion) in background.

Sikorsky HH-3E Jolly Green Giant - Danang Air Base 1968

CH-47 crews returning from a mission, Danang Air Base 1968

Sikorsky HH-3E Jolly Green Giant - Danang Air Base 1968

The flying crane.

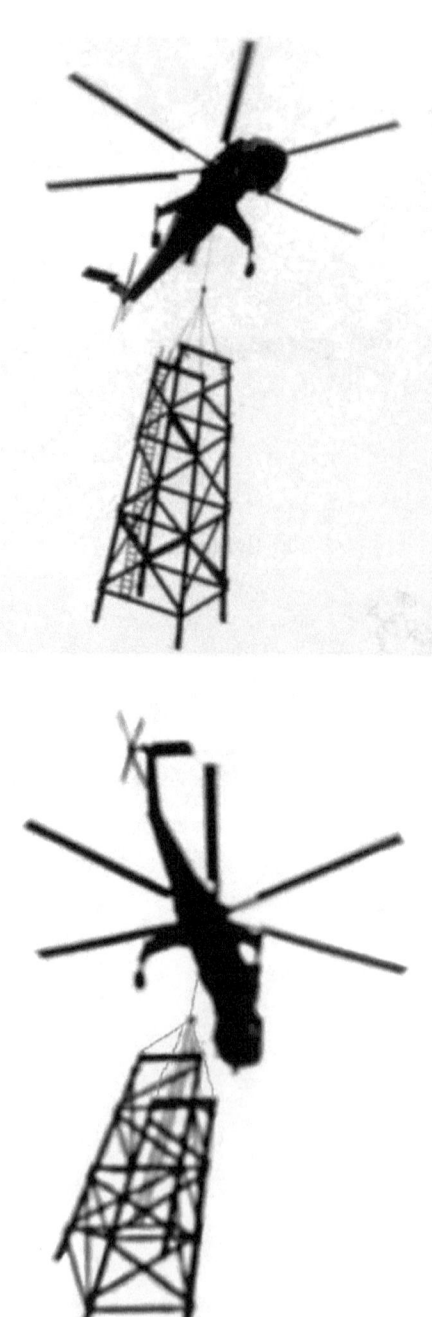

08/12/2010

Name: Thomas H. (Tom) Dunaway, US Army
Location: Foxworth, Mississippi

Comments: I was stationed with the 156th HEM at Marble Mountain, Da Nang, on May 5, 1968, when we were attacked by a 122 mm rocket that hit our tent. Five men were killed, I was the only one standing up within 40 feet of the rocket impact and was not wounded physically but still suffer memories and nightmares from having to pick up body parts after that. Interested in hearing from other vets in the 156th during May 1968. My MOS was 34G20 Field Artillery Digital Automatic Computer (FADAC) repairman. Was sent first to Pleiku to a signal unit, by mistake, stayed there for one month, then on to Da Nang, another mistake, stayed there for about a month, then to Phu Bai to the 578th LEM for 9 months TDY.

CH- 47 crews returning from a mission, Danang Air Base 1968

CH 47's.

We're heading toward Monkey Mountain.
Snapping photos can be risky.

2/17/1998
Name: Mike Kays
From Kentucky

Comments: Sixth Battalion, Seventy-Seventh Artillery, attached to the Twenty-Fifth Infantry Division. Was in Vietnam in 1968. Basecamp was Cu Chi. July '68 was attached to the Ninth Infantry. Towed a 105 mm howitzer unit. Spent time around Trang Bang, Can Tho, Vinh Long, and Quang Tri. Trying to find some of the guys I served with: Coppie, Frenchi, Turner. Mind is starting to slip, can't remember names. Any help appreciated.

The road from China Beach to Camp Tien Sha, Vietnam 1968

Getting close to Monkey Mountain.

Triangle Ammo Dump.

Vietnamese hospital.

Strange neighborhoods.

Gas and Tire station.

Refugee camp.

A church?

Number 10. In Vietnam number 1 meant good and number 10 meant bad. This boy at a rufugee camp is saying number 10 as our crew passes by

In Vietnam number ten means bad.

Scarred survivors.

Frustrated juveniles.

No resting place.

Living conditions, Tien Sha Peninsula
Vietnam 1968

Families gather,,Tien Sha Peninsula - Vietnam 1968

The Vietnamese had deep family
bonds, and repected their elders.

Adults and children having a lot to talk about.

It was good to see that some childred had adults to care for them.

There were many groups of orphan children during the Vietnam war, left to care for themselves.

Small women with heavy loads

Main Entrance - Camp Tien Sha
at the base of Monkey Mountain, Vietnam 1968

Main gate, Camp Tien Sha.

Radar Dishes on Monkey Mountain above Camp Tien Sha Vietnam 1068

10-Jul-2012
Name: Daniel Corcoran

Comments: I was on land assignment about a year, late 1966 to 1967, in Camp Tien Sa, Da Nang—at the base of Monkey Mountain. Fixing radios and electronics. Twelve on, twelve off. Climbed up into my top bunk one night after getting off duty and having a few beers, and a *ground ape* was already on it. Chased him out with the help of other guys in bunks (so I wouldn't shoot the ape instead), fell into bunk, and went to sleep. Next morning, swollen all over, covered in welts and bites from the ape's fleas and lice, ended up in infirmary for 3 days. Does anyone remember me from that incident? Please get in touch! Dan

A busy place,
Camp Tien Sha Vietnam 1968

05/20/2009

Name: Dick Corn, Navy
Location: Grass Valley, California

Comments: APL5 Da Nang in November '67, then TSP Security Sec. 2 from January '67 to November '68. Uprising by black sailors at Tien Sha after Martin Luther King was shot. A TSP security guard was killed by them. Sec. 2 was sent on patrol in search of them. The whole story was swept under the rug by the Navy. Nineteen sixty-eight was a bad year in the 'Nam. Welcome home to all who served.

Mail chopper.

12/05/2009
Name: Alan Lee Harris

Location Miami, Florida

Comments: Seeking information about three incidents at NSA Da Nang, small-craft repair facility. Witnessed the rocket attack on LCU-1477 and YFU-78 as a ship fitter, and as a RT forklift operator, was there and retrieved jawbone with few teeth for ID purposes.

Saw the killing of two white Navy personnel at SCRF as petty officer of the watch-roving patrol. When black militants killed a guard at Camp Tien Sha and made their way to SCRF, surrounded the two white Navy personnel, and killed them, I was notified that I could shoot to kill. Marines in 6Xs arrived with dogs and surrounded and arrested the militants and placed them on their stomachs with their hands behind their heads, about 20 or more in number.

A Navy diver was killed while placing charges on a boat when two personnel boarded the boat and started the engines. The safety line wrapped around the screw, drowning him. I had brought him the evening before into Son Sha village for the evening, and he had told me the only books he ever read were the Bible and the dictionary. When I returned to SCRF to see him, he was underwater with a safety line tender when the two personnel boarded the vessel, and by the time I got on board to tell them to shut down the engines, it was too late. Anyone who knows of this incident and his name, contact me. I have more information.

The third occurrence was when zappers infiltrated the ammo depot and it blew up for three days and nights. Anyone remember this incident?

Inside of barracks, pretty decent living conditions.

The front of our barrack, Camp Tien Sha, BLDG 4.

01/24/2011

Name: Rev Dave Sawley, US Navy
Location: Blanchard, Idaho

Comments: I was at CTS from March '68–February '69 at Public Works. My boss was EM1 Walt Mays. The women who worked for us cleaned up job sites, shops, warehouses, etc. They were age 18 to about 60. While there, we built a new fence around the camp and worked on a lot of other projects.

used with permission of Stanley Houlberg Jr.

2000-01-26
Name: George Lowther
From Austin, Texas

Comments: Great photos! I especially like the "real" China Beach photos.

I was at NSA Da Nang in '66 and '67. I was the radioman on the YFU-67. It was a cargo craft that could travel at blistering speeds of up to 18 knots if the wind was with us. One night we actually had to turn around and return to Da Nang Harbor. The wind was too strong, and we were going backwards—with all three engines full ahead. We carried cargo, ammo, personnel, etc., from Da Nang to Hue and Dong Ha.

I wonder if anyone has ever heard of Tiger Island, in the South China Sea, just north of the Cua Viet River mouth. We had gone too far north that morning (December 18, 1966) and exchanged rounds with an NVA shore battery. They had artillery and mortars; we had two 20 mm machine guns (and small arms). Nothing serious hit us, and we did make it back to the Cua Viet.

The photos of Tien Sha, Monkey Mountain, Bridge Ramp, etc., brought back some memories. Any photos of the White Elephant in Da Nang? A point of interest: Roger Staubach (Dallas Cowboys) was stationed at the White Elephant in Da Nang during that time ('66 and '67). I never saw him, but I heard a lot about him.

Thank you! Great photos!

George

Deep Water Pier.

A couple of gun boats tucked away.

1/31/2013
Name: Paul Mears

Comments: I was at Camp Tien Sha 1968–1969 with Tien Sha Security (TSP) charged with perimeter security. We experienced rocket attacks and long, tedious watches. The ammo dump got hit and went off for days; 500 lb. bombs make quite a racket.

In-country R&R at China Beach surfing the waves and watching the big red Asian sun come up out of the China Sea. Ron Washington was a pal who worked hard for his race. Fellow security pals were "Big Jim" Kelly from New York, Paul Sustin from El Lay, and many others. I would love to hear from anyone at that time.

We guarded the Deep Water Piers and many towers to safeguard our fellow servicemen. I'm proud to have served and grateful to all the vets who answered their country.

Camp Tien Sha at the base of Monkey Mountain. Republic of South Vietnam, 1968

We're heading up Monkey Mountain and looking back at Camp Tien Sha.

06/10/2010

Name: Nhan Thanh Hong, ARVN
Location: Soc Trang, Vietnam

Comments: I was in Da Nang in 1970, first in Da Nang ICS site, the US Thirty-Seventh Signal Battalion, as a detached ARVN Signal Corps soldier for on-site training. Late 1971, I was transferred to Monkey Mountain ICS site (known as Tropo), a site on the side of the mountain. I was staying there to see all US troops withdrawing, the compounds some taken over by ARVN, some left abandoned, later until I ran away from the coming of NVA tanks on 29 of March 1975. I returned on the fireworks displaying night of March 28, 2010, climbing on the hill the next day up to the old site of the AFVN.

Looking back toward China Beach and Marble Mountain.

View from Monkey Mountain overlooking
China Beach and Marble Mountain

Popular landmark on Monkey Mountain.

Looking across Da Nang Harbor towards Nam O
Bridge with raging battles day and night

Monkey Mountain Officers Club over looking
Danang Harbor, Marine compound in forground.

I think this was an officers' club.

Da Nang Harbor.

Monkey Mountain Jet crash

08/04/2005
Name: Steven A. Vaughn, USMC
Location: Monkey Mountain, Da Nang, Republic of Vietnam

Comments: As a young Marine at MAG-11 H&MS-11 I watched a F-8 Crusader make an emergency landing at the Da Nang airstrip. It had a small tree hanging off the stabilizer (tail section). The tree was about 15–20 feet in length. This plane was one of two that had got in trouble at Monkey Mountain that day. We were told the other plane had nosed in just below the crest of the mountain. The pilot had ejected safely and had landed on the beach about 1,200 feet below the crash site.

I was one of those Marines who were sent to the site the next day to salvage as much as we could. I was out of the hydraulic shop at H&MS-11 there with people from Avionics, Airframes and Safety and Survival. I recall 4 of us in the back of the 6x6, the driver and a gunnery sergeant in the cab. We departed the compound, drove through Da Nang, and up the winding road passed the AFRTS broadcasting site to just about 100 yards below a Marine SAM site.

This crash was caused by low visibility through the clouds surrounding Monkey Mountain that morning. The clouds had cleared around the mountain giving about a quarter-mile visibility. The surviving plane had gone into afterburner and just cleared the crest taking with it a little vegetation. The crashed plane pilot had ejected and survived. Now that's the rest of the story.

This jet crashed on Monkey Mountain March 12th 1968.
This pipe line, cables and bunkers were destroyed.

Name: Rick Harris, US Navy

Comments: I am writing to set the record straight concerning the caption accompanying the *Jet Crash on Monkey Mountain*. I was stationed at the small-craft repair facility in Da Nang from August 1968 to August 1969, and during my tour I saw and photographed the F-8 sticking out of Monkey Mountain. This past spring I started searching the Internet in hopes of learning how it got there. I learned that at least two F-8s hit Monkey Mountain: one was the Navy jet that appears on your web site and the other was a Marine Corp plane. The following is what I have learned from those who were involved.

The Navy F-8 (BuNo 150306) that buried itself into the top of the ridge on Monkey Mountain was flown by Lt. Jerry Weber (Ref. 2) of VF-53. According to Jerry's flight log, the crash occurred on 12 March 1968. Jerry and his lead pilot, Lt. Rick Harris (Ref. 1), were diverted to Da Nang after an uneventful BARCAP off Haiphong. Weather had prevented the two Crusader pilots, along with several others, from recovering aboard the *Bon Homme Richard*, and although conditions weren't much better ashore, at least the runway at Da Nang wasn't pitching and rolling.

Jerry's radio and TACAN had gone out so he had to follow Rick. Rick's TACAN wouldn't hold a lock sufficiently to shoot an approach. So Rick decided their best option was to let down though the cloud cover over the South China Sea well to the east of Da Nang and make a visual approach to the south end of Da Nang. The ragged ceiling was forcing the two Crusaders lower and lower, so at 800 feet Rick decided to climb back above the clouds for another try.

As Rick tells it, he was concentrating on his instruments when he encountered a major "tree" head on. The impact tore up the nose and leading edges of Rick's plane pretty bad, but he was still flying. Rick said that when he broke through the cloud cover he saw Jerry was no longer with him was more terrifying than the ride through the trees. Jerry had his own encounter with the trees on Monkey Mountain. As his plane started to lose power and roll over, Jerry grabbed the face curtain and ejected.

Rick wasn't, as they say, out of the woods yet; his close encounter with that major "tree" pushed his instrument panel and radar head almost into his lap. If Rick had tried to eject under those circumstances, he would have left his legs on the underside of the instrument panel. Because of the damage done to his plane, an Air Force pilot had to lead Rick down for a landing approach.

While the first sea-air rescue (SAR) helo was able to talk to Jerry over his survival radio, they had trouble finding him and had to return to Da Nang to refuel. Another helo arrived, and Jerry fired a flare. The helo crew lowered a jungle penetrator to pluck him from the side of Monkey Mountain. After a medical exam and treatment for his cuts and bruises, Jerry was reunited with his flight leader, Rick. Rick told me that seeing Jerry alive and in one piece was one of the greatest moments in his life.

The other F-8 that hit Monkey Mountain belonged to Marine squadron VMFA (AW)-235 a.k.a. "the Death Angels." This one crashed in late summer of 1966. The pilot on its last flight was Captain Ed "Panatella" Kowalczyk, and Patrick "Banshee" Jones (Ref. 3) was his wingman. They launched as a section from Da Nang each with 2 1,000 lb. bombs under the wing.

After takeoff while Ed was lowering his wing, Ed informed Pat that his hydraulics and fire warning lights were lit up. Ed declared an emergency and headed out to sea. Pat cleared the area below him so Ed could jettison his bombs. Ed then raised his wing and lowered his gear to slow down for the impending ejection. Pat still had his ordnance but dirtied up with Ed flying his wing. Pat was wallowing around in and out of burner trying to maintain position. When Ed told Pat he was getting out, Pat took a loose position and watched him leave the airplane.

Pat said he recalls it looked as everything was happening in slow motion. They were about at 2,000 feet since Ed's aircraft was not responding to control or power inputs. Pat watched the seat separate, and after what seemed a long time, Ed separated and then a good chute. Pat was talking to Da Nang tower throughout, and SAR was on the

way. Pat watched Ed drift down to the water and saw what he thought
were local fishermen making their way to Ed.

At about this time Ed's F-8, now a pilotless drone, did a 180 and
was headed straight back to Da Nang with a full load of fuel on board.
Now Pat was in deep kimchee; he couldn't jettison his ordnance because
of all the traffic on the water beneath him. Pat cleaned and positioned
himself between Da Nang, and the stricken Crusader prepared to try
and shoot it down. But as fate would have it, the wounded bird dropped
a wing and nosed over coming to rest about a third of the wayside of the
southeast quadrant of Monkey Mountain. There was an explosion and
fire. As all good Marines do, Pat continued on their original mission,
which he says was to "kill some trees in the open" up around the DMZ.

Pat was back in Da Nang two years later on another tour, and
while getting checked out in an OV-10, he flew over the crash site
and was surprised to see the tail of Ed's F-8 sticking up proudly with
the markings still very fresh. Pat had originally thought that nothing
would be left after the fire, but was pleasantly surprised to see the red
comet's tail paint job looking as fresh as it did on that fateful day two
years earlier.

This F8 slammed in to mountain upside down, and the force pushed the wings to the tail.

This jet crashed on Monkey Mountain March 12th 1968.
It was off the aricraft carrier USS. Bon Homme Richard (CVA-31).

View from Monkey Mountain overlooking
China Beach, Danang, and Camp Tien Sha

The steep winding road to the top of Monkey Mountain.

Monkey Mountain Vietnam 1968
The final climb was scary as hell.

View of Tien Sha Peninsula
from Monkey Mountain, Vietnam 1968

Final steep and dangerous grade before reaching the top.

Looking towards Red Beach, where our journey began.

This base was located south of the peak of Monkey Mountain, overlooking Danang Harbor and China Beach Monkey Mountain has been renamed Són Trà Mountain.

Monkey Mountain Radar Installation

It came to a point where
there were no more smiles.

Towards the end of my tour,
and I just want to get out of this place.

Going home:

My short timers calender was finally full. I was trapped at Camp Tien
Sha at the base of Monkey Mountain my last few days in Nam.

Triangle ammo dump was exploding non stop blocking the road to
Danang Air base. It kind of sounded like shaking a flat sheet of metal.
It was so loud we had to plug our ears. The ammo dump finally fizzled
out after a few days and we headed for Danang Air Base. Over two

hundred of up gathered outside the terminal. We were without weapons and again in our dress whites. We again felt like sitting ducks.

The Pan-American jet roared to a stop just in front of us. Two set of steps were moved to the opening doors. The back stairs were filled with arriving troops. Departing troops used the front stairs to board the jet. Fuel trucks hustled. The smell of fuel was strong. The 727 was shaking from the loading and unloading troops. The jet was hot and smokey. Jet fuel, cigarette smoke and body odor dominated the air inside.

It took only minutes for the huge jet to unload, load and re-fuel. The wind was from the wrong direction to depart over the ocean. Just the day before a Tigar Air Lines jet was shot down a, killing all including over 200 refugee children. We were to take off on the same flight path. The wind started picking up and it started raining as we taxied to the end of the runway. The jet swung around 180 degrees and the jet engines opened up. There was no pre-flight check. It was hammer down, full thrust. I never experienced take off this fast and hard. We lifted off the ground into turbulent wind and rain. We broke thru numerous layers of clouds. Suddenly the jet banked extremely hard. I remember looking down the wing. The wingtip was within a hundred feet of the mountain tops. Looking down you could see Vietnamese waving arms and weapons, and some waving their middle finger. The jet finally gained altitude and cleared the coastline. We cheered with joy knowing we cleared the hostile mountains and were over the ocean.

Our flight home seemed like it took forever. We stopped in the Philippines to refuel for our 18 hour flight to Hawaii. We went thru several sun rises and sun sets. It was a long boring flight but take offs and landing were smooth.

We arrived at Norton Air Force Base on a hot afternoon. We spent several hours at Norton. We were paid and awarded metals and ribbons. We were fed good and treated well by the Military while at Norton. We were then loaded onto busses taking us to LA International Airport.

Hundreds of protestors gathered for our homecoming. Rotten eggs and tomatoes pelted us as we worked our way to the terminal entrance. Police in riot gear engaged the crowd when they tried to get at us. We finally got inside the terminal and out of the reach of protestors. I was lucky enough to have a clean uniform, but some were covered with eggs, tomatoes, and other rancid garbage. I was lucky enough to get a flight to MPLS. We boarded the jet.

I had a 30 day leave. My parents had no idea I was on my way home. I found a flight to Minneapolis, Minnesota. I boarded my flight to Minnesota I just wanted to get home. The lady next to my seat stood up and yelled for a stewardess. A stewardess came, and the lady loudly stated "I'm not going to have my child sitting next to a baby killer". The stewardess intructed me to come with her. I stood up and realized everyone was looking at me. I was ushered to a seat in the back of the jet near the rest rooms. This was a miserable flight with everyone using the bathroom having a sarcastic remark for me.

I finally got to Minneapolis. A friend of mine met me with a private plane, and flew me to my home town in Central Minnesota. I knocked on the front door of my parents home at about 10PM. They had no idea who was knocking that hour of the night. I could of just walked in but wanted to surprise them. My Mom answered the door with my Dad on her heals. My Mom was crying with joy, hugging me and not letting go. I could see a tear in my Dads eye. It felt so good to show them I was OK.

My first day home my parents talked me into wearing my full dress uniform and going to a local American Legion Club with them. We were absolutely shunned. I asked for a beer and was asked for my ID. I wasn't 21 yet so had to drink pop. We were getting dirty looks. We were treated like I had no right to be in that Legion Club. My parents might have been embarrassed by the stares, but they stood tall next me and we're proud of my medals.

This was fall of 1969. Before I left from Vietnam I was given my set of new orders. It was to Adak Alaska, and I turned them down because I didn't want to work in the cold. This would mean I had to keep the next set of orders, which was Iceland.

After spending a quick ending month in Minnesota I had to head out. I had a flight scheduled from Minneapolis to new York then New York to Iceland via Newfoundland and Greenland.

On to Iceland:

I was on leave for 30 days and had orders to Keflavik, Iceland. I turned down my first set of orders to Adak, Alaska. I didn't want duty in a cold climate, so since I could only turn down my orders once, out of the frying pan into the freezer for me.

As an electrician in Reykuvik I had numerous duties. I was a lineman installing and repairing power lines, building and maintained transformer banks, street lights, runway lighting, perimeter lighting, generator operation and repair, changing light bulbs on the water tower, transmission towers and radar dishes. Things would usually break down in bad weather. I often had to work alone at night in a snow storm. Most of the time it was a primary fuse cutout. I had a 60 foot high ranger bucket truck but it was usually too windy to use it, so I had to climb the 45' or 60' poles.

While I was at Keflavik I had the opportunity to take flying lessons. My instructor was Icelandic and spoke very broken English. It was only $13/hr for dual time. Flying over the cliffs on the coast was a rough ride, but I was learning and liked it. On about my 5th lesson the instructor was going to teach me to use the radio. He told me to say "Keflavik tower, this is fox trot lemma echo, landing instructions please". I keyed the mike and nothing came out. I tried it again. I couldn't talk. I froze up. This upset the instructor, and that was my last flying lesson.

I seen the flight surgeon on base. He said he seen this condition before, and told me I can't fly. He gave me a prescription for valium. I was taking 20mg of valium a day for several months, while doing power line work and climbing. I was nervous all the time and couldn't sleep well. I started having nightmares of Vietnam. When in Vietnam rockets and mortars were fired at us almost every night between 2am- 5am. To this day I will wake up at 2am without a sleeping pill.

I finally completed my tour in Iceland. After Iceland I was stationed at the Naval Air Station at Glenview Illinois. They tried me out as a shore patrol. That wasn't for me.

I wanted to be an electrician with my training and experience.

They offered me choice of duty, a pay grade, and about $9,000 to sign four more years as an Electrician Boatman's Mate. That means I would have had to be on a ship, which I could never do, since as a child I would get sick from just riding in a car.

Discharged:

After my tour in Iceland the Navy offered me an $8000 Bonus to reenlist for four more years. The only catch is I would have to become a electrician Boatsman Mate on a ship, since at that time the Seabees were a wartime unit. To stay in the Seabees I would have had to return to Vietnam or other war zone. I didn't want to be on a ship or go back to war so I took and honorable discharge.

One of first places I applied for a job was Burlington Northern. They we're hiring in 1971. I went up to office to fill out an application. This was a large room with people working at about 12 desks.The end of the application asked two questions.

Did you serve in the Military?
Did you serve in Vietnam?

I checked both. I brought the application up to the counter. A secretary carried it to a man in a back office.

He came storming from the back of the room getting every ones attention. He pointed out to me the word Vietnam on my application. He asked me angrily "we're you in Vietnam?

I told him yes. He slammed his fist on the counter and ripped up my application. As I left the room, he shouted "we don't hire Vietnam Veterans here". It was fortunate I was never hired, since the working conditions at Burling Northern send the most employees to the grave in there 50's or early 60's.

I then tried the IBEW.
(International Brothers of Electrical Workers)

They wouldn't give me any credit for my electrical training and experience. They told me I would have to go to school for 18 months to be accepted as an apprentice. During the same time prison inmates could get credit for training.

Discharged:

I received an honorable discharge in October of 1970. I felt really good to be free. I looked forward to getting a good job as an electrician and live the American dream.

It was not to be. I was slandered and ridiculed everywhere I went. I was called a baby killer and looser. Legion and VFW clubs would not accept me.

By January I was a nervous wreck. I couldn't sleep. I felt like the failure and looser I was portrayed to be. I couldn't get a job. Even my parents didn't understand and wouldn't let me live at home. I was homeless, living in my car.

I had no friends or anyone I could talk to. I was going to kill myself to end the pain.

I had enough sense to try the VA. I contact my parents on a cold winter night, and told them to take me to the VA hospital. My Dad dropped me off at the front door of the VA at about 11 PM. He couldn't have helped me anymore than that. After about a half hour of pushing on an after hours button and pounding on the front door of the door an aid finally appeared and let me in. I was cold, deprived of sleep, hungry, thirsty, and just wanted to die.

I ended up in pj's in a lock ward. They started pouring on the drugs.

Drugs like thorazine did nothing but drain my energy. I could barley walk. I learned what the thorazine shuffle was. I was administered my pills twice a day.

The nurse would check your mouth to make sure you swallowed them. If you didn't take your drugs aids would wrestle you to the ground and give you a shot.

If you were combative they would put you in a straight jacket or locked in a padded room.

Therapy and testing began after a few days. I remember sitting on a chair instructed to slam a plastic bat onto a mattress saying "I won't", "I won't".

To this day I don't know what this was about. I won't what? Interacting with other patients helped me a lot. I knew I was not the only one who had the same problems coping with civilian life. I was finally counseled by kind and compassionate doctors. They understood my feelings.

One thing that really scared me was shock treatment. I was getting to know a patient from Big Lake. He was from prominent family. We played cribbage and made plans for the future once we were released. Tim and I were playing cribbage when a nurse and aid showed up and escorted him away. I told we would finish the game when he got back. He had no idea where he was going. An aid walked him back into the ward about a half hour later. He had a fat lip and red bruise on the side of his temple. He had a blank stare and didn't talk. He was escorted to his bed. I snuck bad to his bed where he was laying on his side with a blind stare. He wouldn't talk. A nurse noticed me by him and told me to stay away from him. Later that day he was taken out of my ward. I never seen him again. A few months later I read his obituary. I know of him and three others that had shock treatment. They all killed themselves. One stabbed himself to death in the chest. One hung himself. One shot himself. I don't know how Tim ended his life. I was lucky enough not to be chosen for shock treatment.

I just recently talked to an aid who worked in a lock ward at the VA in 72. He refused to escort fellow veterans to shock treatment. He said he seen lives destroyed right in front of him. Some died in front of him while being shocked. They transferred him to dietetics, a job he could only handle for one day.

He was a special forces black barrette. He lives in seclusion, yet today.

Some employees enjoyed seeing patients get shock treatment. They joked and laughed about it.

Counseling and drug treatment helped me regain some of my will to live.

I was prescribed 40mg of valium a day for what they called nervousness and qualudes so I could sleep. I was rated 10% disabled for nervousness.

I was released from the VA after about five weeks. The first thing I did was contact the American Brotherhood of Electrical workers. I talked to a Union official. I told him I had 18 weeks of schooling and 3 years of lineman experience, plus my own tools. He told me the IBEW gave no credit for military training or experience. He said I had to take a 18 month Electrical training course to get into the Union as an apprentice. I tried for many years to get a job as a union electrician. The last time I tried was 1985. I applied with the IBEW again. I had to go to my high school and get my transcript. They didn't want to see my discharge papers or talk about military training. They didn't want to hear about my 2 years maintenance experience at a meat packing plant. They again advised me I had to go to school. At that time electrical training in prison could be used, but not military training. The IBEW contractors get government contracts, yet they care nothing about veterans.

Another place I applied for a job was Burlington Northern. They were hiring in 1971 when I applied. I walked up a long flight of outside stairs and entered a large office with people working at about 12 desks. A friendly receptionist handed me an application. I filled it out. I noticed the end of the application asked two questions. Did you serve in the Military? Did you serve in Vietnam? I checked both. I presented my application at the counter. A secretary skimmed over it and gave me a look of disgust. She carried it to a man in a back office. He came storming from the back of the room getting everyone's attention. He pointed out to me the word Vietnam on my application. He asked me angrily "were you in Vietnam?" I said yes. He slammed his fist on the counter and ripped up my application. As I left the room, he shouted we don't hire baby killers here. It was fortunate I was never hired, since the working conditions at Burlington Northern send the most employees to the grave in there 50's or early 60's.

I applied for numerous jobs and could only find seasonal construction work. I worked bridge construction as a laborer, carpenter, or iron worker. I was a boomer and had to go where the work was. I lived in my van a lot or rented a room. I never really had a home. I drove to Phoenix my first+ winter. I thought I might get work there but at that time they didn't like snow birds. I didn't dare let anyone know I was a veteran. I came back after a few months. There was always construction work in Minnesota.

I went local college for several quarters. I wasn't sure what to major in.

I getting general education credits out of the way. I had a social science class.

I gave a slide presentation of Vietnam for several large groups of students. The students treated me rudely. They asked me questions like "did you have to kill anyone?". The women shunned me and the men tried to bully me. I had to defend myself several times. I knew I could never attend that college again. This was a time when the Vietnam conflict was still going. Students we're protesting the Vietnam war, and protested me for being at their school.

I moved to Alaska in 77. I had some friends and job leads. My dad was in really bad health at that time. I was hoping I could surprise him by calling from Alaska to tell him I found work. It was a troublesome 6 day drive to Anchorage. I called home to find out my father passed away the day after I left. I missed his funeral. It hurts to this day.

I did find work as a carpenter and electrician. I should have stayed their but something was wrong. I couldn't sleep. The nightmares started again. I was worried about my Mom alone in our family home. Thier was also a close woman friend that told me I had a son.

I decided to go home. I flew back to Minnesota.

The first time I held my infant son he beamed back with a huge smile. Suddenly I was in love, with my son and his mother. We got married and were blessed with a daughter a year later. Life was normal now. I had some sense of purpose in life.

The GI Bill made it possible for me to get more education and make more money in the construction trades. Long haul truck driving was lonely and I missed being with my family and seeing my kids grow. I was gone for weeks at a time. I never was lucky enough to have a good steady job.

Quotes, Facts, Myths, and Realities of the Vietnam War

General Giap was a brilliant, highly respected leader of the North Vietnam military.

The following quote is from his memoirs currently found in the Vietnam war memorial in Hanoi:

What we still don't understand is why you Americans stopped the bombing of Hanoi. You had us on the ropes. If you had pressed us a little harder, just for another day or two, we were ready to surrender! It was the same at the battle of TET. You defeated us! We knew it, and we thought you knew it. But we were elated to notice your media was helping us. They were causing more disruption in America than we could in the battlefields. We were ready to surrender. You had won!' General Giap has published his memoirs and confirmed what most Americans knew. The Vietnam war was not lost in Vietnam– it was lost at home. The same slippery slope, sponsored by the US media, is currently underway. It exposes the enormous power of a Biased Media to cut out the heart and will of the American public.

A truism worthy of note:... Do not fear the enemy, for they can take only your life.

Fear the media, for they will destroy your honor.

Quotes

No event in American history is more misunderstood than the Vietnam War. It was misreported then, and it is misremembered now. Rarely have so many people been so wrong about so much. Never have the consequences of their misunderstanding been so tragic. (Nixon)

The Vietnam War has been the subject of thousands of newspaper and magazine articles, hundreds of books, and scores of movies and television documentaries. The great majority of these efforts have erroneously portrayed many myths about the Vietnam War as being facts. (Nixon)

The Facts Are

91% of Vietnam veterans say they are glad they served. (Westmoreland)

74% said they would serve again even knowing the outcome. (Westmoreland)

There is no difference in drug usage between Vietnam veterans and nonveterans of the same age group (from a Veterans Administration study). (Westmoreland)

Isolated atrocities committed by American soldiers produced torrents of outrage from antiwar critics and the news media while Communist atrocities were so common that they received hardly any attention at all. The United States sought to minimize and prevent attacks on civilians while North Vietnam made attacks on civilians a centerpiece of its strategy. Americans who deliberately killed civilians received prison sentences while Communists who did so received commendations. From 1957 to 1973, the National Liberation Front assassinated 36,725 South Vietnamese and abducted another 58,499. The death squads focused on leaders at the village level and on anyone who improved the lives of the peasants such as medical personnel, social workers, and schoolteachers. Atrocities—every war has atrocities. War is brutal and not fair. Innocent people get killed. (Nixon)

Vietnam Veterans are less likely to be in prison—only 1/2 of one percent of Vietnam Veterans have been jailed for crimes. (Westmoreland)

97% were discharged under honorable conditions; the same percentage of honorable discharges as ten years prior to Vietnam. (Westmoreland)

85% of Vietnam Veterans made a successful transition to civilian life. (McCaffrey)

Vietnam veterans' personal income exceeds that of our nonveteran age group by more than 18 percent. (McCaffrey)

Vietnam veterans have a lower unemployment rate than our nonveteran age group. (McCaffrey)

87% of the American people hold Vietnam Vets in high esteem. (McCaffrey)

Myth: Most Vietnam veterans were drafted.

2/3 of the men who served in Vietnam were volunteers. 2/3 of the men who served in World War II were drafted. (Westmoreland)

Approximately 70% of those killed were volunteers. (McCaffrey)

Myth: The media have reported that suicides among Vietnam veterans range from 50,000 to 100,000—6 to 11 times the non-Vietnam veteran population.

Mortality studies show that 9,000 is a better estimate. "The CDC Vietnam Experience Study Mortality Assessment showed that during the first 5 years after discharge, deaths from suicide were 1.7 times more likely among Vietnam veterans than non-Vietnam veterans. After that initial post-service period, Vietnam veterans were no more likely to die from suicide than non-Vietnam veterans. In fact, after the 5-year post-service period, the rate of suicides is less in the Vietnam veterans' group." (Houk)

Myth: A disproportionate number of blacks were killed in the Vietnam War.

86% of the men who died in Vietnam were Caucasians, 12.5% were black, 1.2% were other races. (CACF and Westmoreland)

Sociologists Charles C. Moskos and John Sibley Butler, in their recently published book *All That We Can Be*, said they analyzed the claim that blacks were used like cannon fodder during Vietnam "and can report definitely that this charge is untrue. Black fatalities amounted to 12 percent of all Americans killed in Southeast Asia—a figure proportional to the number of blacks in the US population at the time and slightly lower than the proportion of blacks in the Army at the close of the war." (*All That We Can Be*)

Myth: The war was fought largely by the poor and uneducated.

Servicemen who went to Vietnam from well-to-do areas had a slightly elevated risk of dying because they were more likely to be pilots or infantry officers.

- 50,000 American servicemen served in Vietnam between 1960 and 1964.
- 9,087,000 military personnel served on active duty during the official Vietnam era (August 5, 1964–May 7, 1975).
- 3,403,100 (including 514,300 offshore) personnel served in the Southeast Asia Theater (Vietnam, Laos, Cambodia, flight crews based in Thailand, and sailors in adjacent South China Sea waters).
- 7,484 American women served in Vietnam. 6,250 were nurses.
- 8 nurses died; 1 was killed in action.
- Vietnam Veterans represented 9.7% of their generation.
- 240 men were awarded the Medal of Honor during the Vietnam era.
- Hostile deaths: 47,378.
- Nonhostile deaths: 10,800.
- Missing in action: 2,338.
- POWs: 766 (114 died in captivity).
- Wounded in action: 303,704.
- Severely disabled: 75,000–23,214 100% disabled; 5,283 lost limbs; 1,081 sustained multiple amputations.
- Married men killed: 17,539.
- Men under the age of 21 killed: 61%.
- Average age of men killed: 22.8 years.

- Highest political office attained by a Vietnam veteran to date: Vice President Al Gore.
- Most successful Vietnam veteran/businessman to date: Frederick Smith of Federal Express.
- 79% of the men who served in Vietnam had a high school education or better when they entered the military service.
- The suicide rate of Vietnam veterans has always been well within the 1.7% norm of the general population.
- 97% of Vietnam-era veterans were honorably discharged. ("Myth vs. Reality" by B. G. Burkett and Glenna Whitley)

Five men killed in Vietnam were only 16 years old. (CACF)

The oldest man killed was 62 years old. (CACF)

11,465 KIAs were less than 20 years old. (CACF)

Vietnam Veterans represent 9.7% of their generation.[†]

8,744,000 GIs were on active duty during the war (August 5, 1964–March 28, 1973).[†]

2,594,000 personnel served within the borders of South Vietnam (January 1, 1965–March 28, 1973).[†]

Another 50,000 men served in Vietnam between 1960 and 1964.[†]

Of the 2.6 million, between 1 and 1.6 million (40–60%) either fought in combat, provided close support, or were at least fairly regularly exposed to enemy attack.[†]

Peak troop strength in Vietnam: 543,482 (April 30, 1969).[†]

Total draftees (1965–1973): 1,728,344.[†]

Draftees accounted for 30.4% (17,725) of combat deaths in Vietnam.[†]

National Guard: 6,140 served; 101 died.[†]

Last man drafted: June 30, 1973.[†]

97% of Vietnam veterans were honorably discharged.[†]

91% of actual Vietnam War–era veterans and 90% of those who saw heavy combat are proud to have served their country.[†]

66% of Vietnam veterans say they would serve again if called upon.[†]

Non-substantiated comments:

Men often had to explain why they served; not serving was acceptable to many.

Soldiers served a tour of duty rather than for the length of the war.

In combat, there was no safety in the rear; there was no rear in Vietnam.

The war was fought in a country whose history, culture, religions, and values were little known or understood by the general population of the United States.

There was no direct threat against the United States.

War against Vietnam was never declared by Congress; thus the correct term is Vietnam Conflict, although the word *war* is commonly used.

The war's goal was unclear; there was never clear indication that America would do whatever was necessary to win.

There were no clear combat zones; there was no front.

Territory was taken, lost, and taken repeatedly.

Little emotional support was offered to soldiers returning home.

All of the soldiers did not return home at the same time.

No war since the Civil War caused such a rift in US public opinion, leading to social unrest and violence.

The war was broadcast on television daily. It has been called the television war.

Myth: The average age of an infantryman fighting in Vietnam was 19.

Assuming KIAs accurately represented age groups serving in Vietnam, the average age of an infantryman (MOS 11B) serving in Vietnam to be 19 years old is a myth; it is actually 22.8. None of the enlisted grades have an average age of less than 20. (CACF)

The average man who fought in World War II was 26 years of age. (Westmoreland)

Myth: The domino theory was proved false.

The domino theory was accurate. The ASEAN (Association of Southeast Asian Nations) countries—Philippines, Indonesia, Malaysia, Singapore, and Thailand—stayed free of Communism because of the US commitment to Vietnam. The Indonesians threw the Soviets out in 1966 because of America's commitment in Vietnam. Without that commitment, Communism would have swept all the way to the Malacca

Straits that is south of Singapore and of great strategic importance to the free world. If you ask people who live in these countries that won the war in Vietnam, they have a different opinion from the American news media. The Vietnam War was the turning point for Communism. (Westmoreland)

Democracy catching on. In the wake of the Cold War, democracies are flourishing, with 179 of the world's 192 sovereign states (93%) now electing their legislators, according to the Geneva-based Inter-Parliamentary Union. In the last decade, 69 nations have held multiparty elections for the first time in their histories. Three of the five newest democracies are former Soviet republics: Belarus (where elections were first held in November 1995), Armenia (July 1995), and Kyrgyzstan (February 1995). And two are in Africa: Tanzania (October 1995) and Guinea (June 1995). (Parade Magazine)

Myth: The fighting in Vietnam was not as intense as in World War II.

The average infantryman in the South Pacific during World War II saw about 40 days of combat in four years. The average infantryman in Vietnam saw about 240 days of combat in one year thanks to the mobility of the helicopter.

One out of every 10 Americans who served in Vietnam was a casualty. 58,169 were killed and 304,000 wounded out of 2.59 million who served. Although the percent who died is similar to other wars, amputations or crippling wounds were 300 percent higher than in World War II. 75,000 Vietnam veterans are severely disabled. (McCaffrey)

Medevac helicopters flew nearly 500,000 missions. Over 900,000 patients were airlifted (nearly half were American). The average time lapse between wounding to hospitalization was less than one hour. As a result, less than one percent of all Americans wounded who survived the first 24 hours died.

The helicopter provided unprecedented mobility. Without the helicopter it would have taken three times as many troops to secure the 800 mile border with Cambodia and Laos (the politicians thought the Geneva Conventions of 1954 and the Geneva Accords or 1962 would secure the border). (Westmoreland)

The 1990 unsuccessful movie *Air America* helped to establish the myth of a connection between Air America, the CIA, and the Laotian drug trade. The movie and a book the movie was based on contend that the CIA condoned a drug trade conducted by a Laotian client. Both agree that Air America provided the essential transportation for the trade, and both view the pilots with sympathetic understanding. American-owned airlines never knowingly transported opium in or out of Laos, nor did their American pilots ever profit from its transport. Yet undoubtedly every plane in Laos carried opium at some time, unknown to the pilot and his superiors. For more information see http://www. air-america.org/

Poor job of reporting by the news media.

Facts about the Fall of Saigon

Myth: Kim Phuc, the little nine-year-old Vietnamese girl running naked from the napalm strike near Trang Bang on 8 June 1972, was burned by Americans bombing Trang Bang.

No American had involvement in this incident near Trang Bang that burned Phan Thi Kim Phuc. The planes doing the bombing near the village were VNAF (Vietnam Air Force) and were being flown by Vietnamese pilots in support of South Vietnamese troops on the ground. The Vietnamese pilot who dropped the napalm in error is currently living in the United States. Even the AP photographer Nick Ut, who took the picture, was Vietnamese. The incident in the photo took place on the second day of a three-day battle between the North Vietnamese Army (NVA) who occupied the village of Trang Bang and the ARVN (Army of the Republic of Vietnam) who were trying to force the NVA out of the village. Recent reports in the news media that an American commander ordered the air strike that burned Kim Phuc are incorrect. There were no Americans involved in any capacity. "We (Americans) had nothing to do with controlling VNAF," according to Lieutenant General (Retired) James F. Hollingsworth, the commanding general of TRAC at that time. Also, it has been incorrectly reported that two of Kim Phuc's brothers were killed in this incident. They were Kim's cousins, not her brothers.

Myth: The United States lost the war in Vietnam.

The American military was not defeated in Vietnam. The American military did not lose a battle of any consequence. From a military standpoint, it was almost an unprecedented performance. (Westmoreland quoting Douglas Pike, a professor at the University of California, Berkley, a renowned expert on the Vietnam War)

This included Tet 68, which was a major military defeat for the VC and NVA.

The United States did not lose the war in Vietnam. The South Vietnamese did.

Facts about the End of the War

The fall of Saigon happened 30 April 1975, two years *after* the American military left Vietnam. The last American troops departed in their entirety 29 March 1973. How could we lose a war we had already stopped fighting? We fought to an agreed stalemate. The peace settlement was signed in Paris on 27 January 1973. It called for release of all US prisoners, withdrawal of US forces, limitation of both sides' forces inside South Vietnam, and a commitment to peaceful reunification.*

The 140,000 evacuees in April 1975 during the fall of Saigon consisted almost entirely of civilians and Vietnamese military, *not* American military running for their lives.*

There were almost twice as many casualties in Southeast Asia (primarily Cambodia) the first two years after the fall of Saigon in 1975 than there were during the ten years the US was involved in Vietnam.*

POW-MIA Issue (Unaccounted-for versus Missing in Action)

Politics & People, "On Vietnam, Clinton Should Follow a Hero's Advice," Senator John Kerrey is quoted as saying about Vietnam, there has been "the most extensive accounting in the history of human warfare" of those missing in action. While there are still officially more than 2,200 cases, there now are only 55 incidents of American servicemen who were last seen alive but aren't accounted for. By contrast, there still are 78,000 unaccounted-for Americans from World War II and 8,100 from the Korean conflict.

"The problem is that those who think the Vietnamese haven't cooperated sufficiently think there is some central repository with answers to all the lingering questions," notes Gen. John Vessey, the former chairman of the Joint Chiefs of Staff and the Reagan and Bush administration's designated representative in MIA negotiations. "In all the years we've been working on this, we have found that's not the case."***

More Realities about the War

Post-traumatic stress disorder (PTSD)—it was not invented or unique to Vietnam Veterans. It was called "shell shock" and other names in previous wars. An automobile accident or other traumatic event also can cause it. It does not have to be war related. The Vietnam War helped medical progress in this area.

Restraining the military in Vietnam in hindsight probably prevented a nuclear war with China or Russia. The Vietnam War was shortly after China got involved in the Korean War, the time of the Cuban missile crisis, Soviet aggression in Eastern Europe and the proliferation of nuclear bombs. In all, a very scary time for our country.

Sources

[Nixon] *No More Vietnams* by Richard Nixon.

[*Parade Magazine*] August 18, 1996 page 10.

[CACF] Combat Area Casualty File November 1993 (The CACF is the basis for the Vietnam Veterans Memorial, i.e., The Wall), Center for Electronic Records, National Archives, Washington, DC.

[*All That We Can Be*] *All That We Can Be* by Charles C. Moskos and John Sibley Butler

[Westmoreland] Speech by General William C. Westmoreland before the Third Annual Reunion of the Vietnam Helicopter Pilots Association (VHPA) at the Washington, DC, Hilton Hotel on July 5, 1986 (reproduced in a Vietnam Helicopter Pilots Association Historical Reference Directory Volume 2A).

[McCaffrey] Speech by Lt. Gen. Barry R. McCaffrey (reproduced in *The Pentagram*, June 4, 1993), assistant to the Chairman of the Joint Chiefs of Staff, to Vietnam veterans and visitors gathered at "The Wall," Memorial Day 1993.

[Houk] Testimony by Dr. Houk, Oversight on Post-Traumatic Stress Disorder, July 14, 1988, page 17, hearing before the Committee on Veterans' Affairs, United States Senate One Hundredth Congress second session. Also "Estimating the Number of Suicides Among Vietnam Veterans" (*American Journal of Psychiatry* 147, 6 June 1990 pages 772–776).

**The Wall Street Journal*, June 1, 1996, page A15.

1996 Information Please Almanac 1995 Information Please Almanac Atlas & Yearbook 49th edition, Houghton Mifflin Company, Boston & New York 1996, pages 117, 161 and 292.

†The Vietnam War Internet Project, an educational organization dedicated to providing information and documents about the various Indochina Wars and to the collection and electronic publication on the web of oral histories and memoirs of both those who served in and those who opposed those conflicts. [HOME PAGE]

"Myth vs. Reality" by B. G. Burkett and Glenna Whitley

Origins of the Vietnam War

In 1941, a Comintern agent named Ho Chi Mihn formed the League for the Independence of Vietnam, better known as the Viet Mihn. This Communist-affiliated force fought against the Japanese, who were actually in control of French Indochina during W WII. While ostensibly administered by Vichy France, Imperial Japan was actually in charge on the ground with French bureaucrats doing their bidding. The OSS (US Office of Strategic Services) aided the Viet Mihn against the Japanese, but the Pentagon correctly saw this theater as a sideshow and refused to commit significant assets.

The Japanese eventually threw out and humiliated the Vichy French officials in the region and gave Vietnam nominal independence in the Greater East Asia Co-Prosperity Sphere. When Japan surrendered, they turned over Vietnam to the Viet Mihn.

The needs of the Cold War showed the US government that France was going to be critical to the vital European theater, so no opposition was launched against French claims in Indochina. The independent Vietnamese government only lasted a few days before the British and Chinese occupied the region and eventually allowed the French to return. Ho Chi Minh used the time to weaken nationalist opposition by assassinations and overt attacks.

Ho Chi Mihn and his followers fled into the mountains and began a guerrilla war as the French reoccupied Indochina, and after the defeat of the Nationalists in China, received aid from the People's Republic of China and USSR. The eight-year war cost the French 94,000 dead and 40,000 captured. The basic French plan was to push the Viet Mihn to attack strong positions in remote locations, where French logistics were superior and the French forces could inflict stinging losses. The French were worn down by shortages of engineer barrier materials, poor road networks, and limited amounts of mobile forces able to respond to each crisis in turn.

While most French actions resulted in victory, each loss was difficult to replace, while the Viet Mihn could afford even the heaviest losses. The French moved from attempts to control all of Indochina to attempts to control secure zones and sweeps outside of those zones. The Viet Mihn increasingly possessed heavy weapons and supporting arms. The new French commander Henri Navarre reported he was unable to produce victory in the war but could still achieve a stalemate. He selected Dien Ben Phu as the site. This was an old Japanese airstrip with loyal tribes in the area. It was less than 10 miles from Laos and less than 200 from Hanoi and was astride the main Viet Mihn supply route deeper south.

The French had missed the transition from guerrilla to mixed warfare, on the lines proposed by Mao, and thus found that at the end of a long supply line, their firepower wasn't as great as that of General Giap. Mixed warfare was the phase when the guerrillas were able to field the beginnings of real armies. The response to guerrillas was to spread out to track them down, but with real army units available, the counter-guerrillas could not spread out without being vulnerable to the army forces, and if they concentrated to face the army, the guerrillas were unmolested. Even with covert US aid to deliver supplies to Dien Ben Phu, the French were unable to keep their forces fully combat ready, and they were eventually defeated one fortification at a time. The Viet Mihn were aided by overt Chinese support and were able to call on vast logistical aid. General Giap praised the performance of his 400 Soviet-supplied GAZ trucks in keeping his forces supplied, even during the monsoon, which crippled French resupply attempts.

This French phase ended with Indochina broken into North and South Vietnam, Laos, and Cambodia. This was a great complication, for the communist forces were always clear they were fighting for Indochina, not a specific country, while the West was hamstrung by international boundaries.

The outbreak of the Korean War finally ended US ambivalence over Vietnam. Now seen as part of the Soviet and Chinese plan to take over the Pacific Rim, US advisors were sent to Vietnam. During the overlapping period while the French were still in Vietnam and Korea was ongoing, March Battalion Korea was sent to fight with the UN forces in Korea, becoming a well-regarded part of the US Second Infantry Division. It was later destroyed in Vietnam.

US Entry into the Vietnam War

Under President Eisenhower a force of 500 instructors was to lead and teach Republic of Vietnam forces. As the unpopular Diem government alienated Buddhists and others, the communist government of the North decided it was time to move, and formed the National Liberation Front, better known as the Vietcong (VC). President Kennedy decided the Vietnamese were incapable of solving the problem on their own, and that US combat forces were required. He sent 12,000 US troops into the fray. The ability of the VC to operate in the south was correctly seen as the first issue to solve, but the strategic hamlet plan to separate the population from the guerrillas was badly handled and served to further anger the peasant farmers, already incensed about high rent payment to landowners.

Kennedy approved the removal of the now hated Diem and his family, though he was shocked when the coup resulted in their deaths. The coup was a strategic error, creating a period of instability, and the NLF quickly took advantage. US forces were increased to 16,000 as Kennedy sought a way to regain control.

The assassination of President Kennedy was followed by President Johnson, who saw Vietnam as a distraction from his domestic priorities. A pair of controversial attacks on USN warships in the waters off Vietnam was used to increase the US commitment to the war. The first of these two attacks certainly took place, and the missile boats are in

Vietnamese museums. The second attack may have been a radar error and remains controversial to this day. Lyndon B. Johnson used these to force a major increase in forces committed, unwilling to be seen as the president who lost the war.

The US started a major bombing campaign against the North to encourage it to stop supporting the NLF, and began increases of military forces committed until US troops topped half a million. Additionally, Filipino, Thai, Australian, New Zealand, and Korean troops also fought for the South.

President Johnson had a very secretive policy and this lack of candor hurt his policy with the US public. Current scholarship is reexamining conventional wisdom about the role of the antiwar movement, but at the time it was seen as a major theater of conflict and a vital means to defeat US involvement in the war. The traditional American weakness in Information Operations was well evident during the whole conflict.

The Tet Offensive

In January of 1968 the NLF attacked Khe Sanh in the Demilitarized Zone in what proved to be the biggest battle of the whole war. Some 10,000 North Vietnamese were killed as well as around 500 US soldiers. It proved to be a diversionary tactic from what was to take place a week later, the Tet Offensive.

On the night of January 31, while the country was celebrating the Lunar New Year, the Vietcong started an enormous offensive on towns and cities all over South Vietnam including Saigon, where the courtyard of the US embassy was briefly occupied. US and South Vietnamese forces hit back with huge firepower which caused huge losses of VC personnel and civilians. Around 3,000 members of the Army of the Republic of Vietnam (ARVN) and US troops lost their lives as a result of the Tet Offensive, while more than 30,000 VC troops were killed.

While US military chiefs claimed a great victory, the shocked media back in the United States portrayed it as a stunning US defeat having seen events unfold on their TV sets. As a result, public opposition to the war back in the United States reached an all-time high. In spite of enormous VC casualties, the Tet Offensive ultimately proved to work in their favor. Antiwar demonstrations in the United States became even more widespread as reports of atrocities against Vietnamese civilians became public, such as the My Lai Massacre.

Final Years of the Vietnam War (1969–75)

One notable casualty of the Tet Offensive was the presidency of Lyndon Johnson, who was succeeded by President Nixon, who was elected in no small part to put an end to the war. When elected, he didn't know how he was going to do this, but his staff quickly put together the Vietnamization program. US units would gradually turn over missions to the ARVN which would be greatly strengthened and trained. As part of this comprehensive restructuring, the government of Cambodia under Sihanouk was forced to abandon their claims of neutrality while sheltering People's Army of Vietnam forces on his soil, and Nixon ordered secret bombing raids on those extranational sanctuaries. Sihanouk was deposed, and the Khmer Rouge were able to take advantage of the instability. Cross-border ground operations took place and were followed by Vietnamese-led incursions into Laos, which served as a sanctuary for the People's Army of Vietnam (PAVN).

US forces continued to draw down, and fell to less than 200,000 in 1971, with more reductions scheduled. Nineteen seventy-two saw overt invasion from the North. US airpower provided the edge needed to defeat the Easter Invasion. Another US aerial attack was used to force the North to negotiate the Paris Peace Accords. US military forces were essentially removed after this, as required within 60 days. This was the only part of the treaty that actually took place.

In 1975, the North again attacked, with more tanks than the Wehrmacht used to invade France in 1940 and more trucks than Patton's Third Army. The critical US logistical and air support was denied. President Thieu panicked and issued a series of conflicting orders to his forces, which collapsed in the face of the invasion.

The Republic of Vietnam fell on April 30, 1975, right after Cambodia fell to the Khmer Rouge and months before Laos fell to the Pathet Lao.

In Vietnam, hundreds of thousands were imprisoned by the new leadership, with tens of thousands killed. Two million fled the country. Two million died in Cambodia alone, almost a third of the population, killed by the Khmer Rouge. In 1995, Hanoi admitted that four million civilians died in the war, North and South, and over a million Vietnamese soldiers. US forces suffered 58,000 dead.

In 1941, a Comintern agent named Ho Chi Mihn formed the League for the Independence of Vietnam, better known as the Viet Mihn. This Communist-affiliated force fought against the Japanese, who were actually in control of French Indochina during W WII. While ostensibly administered by Vichy France, Imperial Japan was actually in charge on the ground with French bureaucrats doing their bidding. The OSS (US Office of Strategic Services) aided the Viet Mihn against the Japanese, but the Pentagon correctly saw this theater as a sideshow, and refused to commit significant assets.

The Japanese eventually threw out and humiliated the Vichy French officials in the region and gave Vietnam nominal independence in the Greater East Asia Co-Prosperity Sphere. When Japan surrendered, they turned over Vietnam to the Viet Mihn.

The needs of the Cold War showed the US government that France was going to be critical to the vital European theater, so no opposition was launched against French claims in Indochina. The independent Vietnamese government only lasted a few days before the British and Chinese occupied the region, and eventually allowed the French to return. Ho Chi Minh used the time to weaken nationalist opposition by assassinations and overt attacks.

Ho Chi Mihn and his followers fled into the mountains and began a guerrilla war as the French reoccupied Indochina, and after the defeat of the Nationalists in China, received aid from the People's Republic of China and USSR. The eight-year war cost the French 94,000 dead and 40,000 captured. The basic French plan was to push the Viet Mihn to attack strong positions in remote locations, where French logistics were superior and the French forces could inflict stinging losses. The French were worn down by shortages of engineer barrier materials, poor road networks, and limited amounts of mobile forces able to respond to each crisis in turn.

While most French actions resulted in victory, each loss was difficult to replace, while the Viet Mihn could afford even the heaviest losses. The French moved from attempts to control all of Indochina to attempts to control secure zones and sweeps outside of those zones. The Viet Mihn increasingly possessed heavy weapons and supporting arms. The new French commander Henri Navarre reported he was unable to produce victory in the war but could still achieve a stalemate. He selected Dien Ben Phu as the site. This was an old Japanese airstrip with loyal tribes in the area. It was less than 10 miles from Laos and less than 200 from Hanoi, and was astride the main Viet Mihn supply route deeper south.

The French had missed the transition from guerrilla to mixed warfare, on the lines proposed by Mao, and thus found that at the end of a long supply line, their firepower wasn't as great as that of General Giap. Mixed warfare was the phase when the guerrillas were able to field the beginnings of real armies. The response to guerrillas was to spread out to track them down, but with real army units available, the counter-guerrillas could not spread out without being vulnerable to the army forces, and if they concentrated to face the army, the guerrillas were unmolested.

Even with covert US aid to deliver supplies to Dien Ben Phu, the French were unable to keep their forces fully combat ready, and they were eventually defeated one fortification at a time. The Viet Mihn were aided by overt Chinese support and were able to call on vast logistical aid. General Giap praised the performance of his 400 Soviet-supplied GAZ trucks in keeping his forces supplied, even during the monsoon, which crippled French resupply attempts. This French phase ended with Indochina broken into North and South Vietnam, Laos, and Cambodia. This was a great complication, for the communist forces were always clear they were fighting for Indochina, not a specific country, while the West was hamstrung by international boundaries.

The outbreak of the Korean War finally ended US ambivalence over Vietnam. Now seen as part of the Soviet and Chinese plan to take over the Pacific Rim, US advisors were sent to Vietnam. During the overlapping period while the French were still in Vietnam and Korea was ongoing, March Battalion Korea was sent to fight with the UN forces in Korea, becoming a well-regarded part of the US Second Infantry Division. It was later destroyed in Vietnam.

Please note that this article was prepared for us by a US journalist. As is the case with all historical writing, interpretation of events may vary.